DIALING STRANGERS

Overcoming Your Hangups and Producing Cold Calls That Sell

DAVE TESTER

Dialing Strangers

ISBN-13: 978-1-938332-05-0

Book Cover by Lee Roesner – Paradigm Graphic Design & Web Development
Book Design by Aspen Kuhlman – SO&SO Co LLC

To book David @ your next speaking engagement, contact him through:
www.dialingstrangers.com

Printed in the United States of America

10 9 8 7 6 5 4 3 2 1

First Edition

The summer of 2001 I was feeling sorry for myself. I was thrown into sales when my contract wasn't renewed for a TV sports anchor job. "What am I going to do?" I worried out loud. My wife said "You're going to put on a suit, get your game face on, go out and own it!" This book is dedicated to the woman who made me see what I couldn't, my wife, Claudia.

I hope this book will help create a new vision of what's possible for you as well. The sales world is tough, but if you dare to learn the concepts, there is great reward ahead for you. I know. It happened to me.

Dave

TABLE OF CONTENTS

INTRODUCTION

The number was 772-4909. You can look it up.

This was the phone number for the biggest cold call of my life.

It was Labor Day weekend 1977. I dialed Shanell's house. She was my sixth-grade crush. I had found her family's telephone number in the phone book and memorized it. Before I could pick up the receiver and actually dial, I spent a grueling hour convincing myself to get up the guts to even try. My stomach did flip flops. My fingers were actually sweating. I dialed: 7-7-2-4-9-0-9 and immediately stopped breathing. It rang once, then twice, and then on the third ring it happened. Her brother—at least, I think it was her brother; I hoped it wasn't her dad—answered. "Hello...Hello?" Somehow I managed to speak, but I barely recognized the sound of my own voice, "Is Shanell there?" "Yeah." I heard him drop the receiver on a hard surface and shout her name. It seemed like an eternity of waiting and waiting and waiting. My heart pounded. I waited. I felt happy and sick at the same time. I waited. I was really going to do it. I was really going to ask her to go to the county fair with me. I kept waiting. Then, my mind raced through a series of tough questions: *What if she says no? What if she laughs at me? What if she makes fun of me? What if I am rejected?* Thirty-six years later, I wonder *what if I hadn't hung up the phone the moment Shanell said hello?* My worries had overcome my ability to function.

Each day as sales professionals, we're asked to pick up the phone and make cold calls that could change our lives—both professionally and personally. Most of us face many of the same universal fears that I faced as a sixth grader: *What if I get rejected? What if I get laughed at? What if I'm made fun of? What if I end up looking stupid?* Surprisingly, most of us—even as adults—have about the same amount of specialized training that I had as a sixth grader—none!

It turns out that many of us enter the sales profession in the exact same way. How? Unsure, unprepared and quite by accident.

My story is like many who find themselves in sales. I got there when I lost my job doing something else. For me personally, I became a sales person quite by accident after a long stint as a TV / radio personality. The transition occurred with little fanfare. After I had spent nearly 1400 hours on television as a nightly news sportscaster, my station manager walked up to me one afternoon and calmly said, "Hey, we aren't doing sports anymore." I responded, "You mean, not tonight?" He replied, "No. I mean not for good... you're fired."

Despite the terrible surprise, I somehow landed on my feet in the professional sales arena. My thought process was incredibly simplistic: *how hard could sales be?* Surely, the transition to sales was a no-brainer. I mean, really, I was already an excellent communicator. My line of thought was validated by my new sales manager. "It's sales! Your job is basically to call people and talk to them. You can talk, right?"

Of course, I could talk. I could talk to a radio microphone or a TV camera to thousands of people at once. And I could make people stop and listen. Obviously, in sales I would be a total natural success. Even my Grandmother told me I had the 'gift of gab.' I was a potential superstar. The sales manager was thrilled to hire me. I was flattered by his encouragement and believed his promises.

Like most accidental sales people, my job training was minimal. So minimal, I almost missed it. My new boss handed me a blank call sheet, threw a thick yellow phone directory at me, and yelled, "Go get 'em kid! It's all about the numbers. Start Dialing for Dollars."

Welcome to the school of hard knocks!

I remember asking a frazzled co-worker, "Did he say, 'Dialing for Dollars'?'"

"Yeah, but he meant 'Dialing for Death.' Good luck."

I didn't figure I needed luck. I scooped up the telephone book, opened it, and picked a random number. But, as soon as I dialed, something horrible happened. I was transported back to 1977. In my mind, I replayed the classic Shanell episode in high-definition slow motion. I immediately started thinking those same old thoughts. *What if I am laughed at?*

What if I am told no? What if I am rejected? I hope no one answers! What if someone says hello?

I tried to find a way to make successful calls, but at that point in my new career, I didn't yet know how. It occurred to me that maybe if I watched what other sales professionals were doing, I could emulate their actions. I watched, but I couldn't decipher how their fractured activities could possibly be parlayed into sales success. Like so many accidental sales people, I began to wonder: *What is wrong with me? Why can't I make this work? Why am I so worried about what other people think?*

Eventually, I gathered up the courage to ask my sales manager the important question that so many first-timers ask: "Is anyone going to help me?" I could distinctly remember that when I was hired I had been promised training. I also had been promised a great lead list. Like many other new sales people, my distinct memory of that promise turned out to be a huge misunderstanding. To me, training meant someone would explain to me how to do my job, answer my questions, and even quiet my fears. To my new company, training meant an opportunity for me to find out for myself how to survive cold calling through unassisted, on-the-job experience.

Oh. Okay. Big misunderstanding.

When I realized that training was not going to happen, I accepted the notion that this tactic must be a key part of how sales people become successful. I blamed the training misunderstanding on myself. I figured I was so new in the arena that I obviously didn't understand how things were done here. In sales, I surmised, training is based on survival of the fittest. The rite of passage must be based on the timeless sink-or-swim technique. Still, the idea didn't make sense on a financial level. Surely, management must want every sales person to have a chance to succeed. I wondered if maybe I was missing something. Then, I remembered the second promise made when I was hired.

The great lead list! I was promised a great lead list. Where is that?

Turns out that the great lead list was a big misunderstanding, too. It was a wish list. I felt sheepish about not knowing how things were done in the high-powered world of sales. I had imagined that the great lead list would be a bunch of well-chosen names and phone numbers hand-picked by my manager. Meanwhile, my new company saw that promise differently. They saw the lead list as an opportunity for me to learn firsthand how to leverage the use of the phone book, the greatest lead list in the world.

My sales manager offered me some age-old advice: "It's a numbers game. Be a good sales soldier. Make your calls. Fill out your weekly call sheet. Trust me, it's all about Dialing for Dollars." (I now know he offered this advice because that's how it had been done in the sales world since beginning of time!)

Fine. I did trust him. I promised to get on the battle-field and do exactly what he suggested. I told myself that the classic Dialing for Dollars strategy was a proven road to success for all sales people. All I had to do was play the numbers game.

I followed that failed sales strategy for as long as I could.

Eventually, I got tired of reliving the sixth grade Shanell moment in my head. I also got tired of real-life prospects and probabilities saying "no" and hanging up on me. **I started finding places to go and hide. Long coffee breaks. Long lunch hours. I started calling friends and family so that I could talk to people who I believed didn't hate me. Then, I dove even deeper and took up the art of writing complete fiction on my call sheet.** It was easier to make up fantasy figures than face the fear of calling real people. I told my manager that I left a message, but no one called me back yet! I started going to the local copy shop and working on my resume. Then I'd decide to give the Dialing for Dollars strategy another run.

It was a vicious circle.

And then one day, in the darkest of dark moments, I found a way out.

For some reason, when I replayed the Shanell incident in my head for the millionth time, I asked myself a different set of what-if questions. *What if I was the only boy who summoned the courage to ask the best-looking girl in elementary school to the county fair? What if I had not hung up the phone when Shanell answered my call? What if I had given her the chance to say yes to me?*

I felt my heart pound.

I had a major epiphany. In all my recent sales calls, I had been haunted by that old fear of rejection. But, the biggest cold call of my life had not actually ended in Shanell's rejection of me. That girl never had a *chance* to reject me—I rejected me. The cold call to her ended when I rejected the biggest opportunity I had ever created for myself.

I couldn't believe the deep relief I felt from that discovery.

Suddenly, a flood of other what-if questions came to me. *What if I stopped repeating that same mistake as an adult? What if I used my television and radio skills to make cold calling fun? What if I paid attention to the tone and tempo of my voice? What if I slowed down? What if I listened up and lightened up?*

Then, I had the biggest what-if thought ever. *What if my sales manager's strategy of Dialing for Dollars was simply wrong?*

As the Dialing for Dollars myth became clearer to me, my whole outlook shifted. I realized that I had practiced the core advice and even achieved the daily behaviors. I had a smile on my face, a product in my pocket, and a suit that looked great on me. I had played the numbers game for days, weeks, and even months at a time. But following the Dialing for Dollars strategy hadn't meant that prospects made an appointment with me or even accepted my call. I replayed the big question in my mind: *What if my sales manager's strategy of Dialing for Dollars was simply wrong? What if I could leverage a way to make fewer calls, make more money, and get more time off?*

I felt a surge of freedom.

What if I created a new method to control the cold call?

I thought hard about the sales information I'd collected. Over the course of my early career—my dialing finger and my psyche weary-- I had been hammered with the belief that sales IS a numbers game. Make one hundred calls a day on the quest to set ten appointments. It takes ten appointments to generate two sales. One in eight people might take a call. Expect as many as 98 rejections out of every 100 calls.

For the first time, I wondered: *What if I am not the kind of human being who can actually survive the Dialing for Dollars level of rejection? What if I am better—and smarter—than that? This was the moment of clarity and relief. My "Aha!" moment!*

I considered the differences between what our sales team was told to do and what most of us actually did. When it came down to the hard facts on cold calling, what we said we did and what we truly did were not often the same. Based on my own observations, the average account executive would make ten dials a day and feel like a failure for not making 100. Out of ten calls, it was likely that five of those calls were focused on prospecting new business. Probably fifty percent of the weekly calls were geared toward talking to current customers, doing what could be described as "professional visiting" which was not asking for money but just talking about nice things like the weather and your favorite team. I estimated that about 80 percent of the opportunities discovered during conversations were never actually followed up on with a return phone call because the numbers game got in the way. Because my sales colleagues and I clung to the Dialing for Dollars mindset, we missed some important opportunities. The goal had actually shifted from making a sale to achieving your dial quota.

I asked myself another round of critical questions. *What if making more and more calls each day was actually the wrong approach? What if the model of step-up and man-up could be transformed into slow down, relax, and make fewer dials in a day? What if 'lighten up and listen up' was the mantra instead? What if I decided when the call was over, not the prospect?* Wow, what a concept!

For the first time since I became an accidental sales person, I genuinely smiled. Forget Dialing for Dollars. It was time to take control of my cold calls. My way. That's when I started developing and perfecting my simple 9-step program for making cold calls – also known as Dialing Strangers.

Developing and practicing cold calls, has transformed my life and sales career forever. Now you can reap the benefits and skip the anxiety. It can change your life, too--from fear to fun!

If you find yourself being forced to make 50 to 100 calls each day and failing, it's because you're following the wrong strategy. If your sales manager's answer to your struggle is 'make more dials' or 'it's a numbers game' or 'pick up the phone and start making calls,' it's time that you find out that there is a better way. If you have been promised a great sales career with fast cars and big houses, lots of training and a long, long list of leads...Well, I promise that you can save yourself years of agony and effort by learning more about the secrets and skills of Dialing Strangers.

Here is the truth: your single most profitable skill as a sales person is your ability to control the cold call. If you don't take control of your sales career, someone else will determine your future. If you do not choose your own plan, you will become part of someone else's plan. Cold calling is your most important asset. This is a method to reach your sales goals, make fewer cold calls, make more money, and enjoy more time off. It's even fun!

Ask Yourself: *What if I didn't try to yell and sell? What if I started feeling good about myself? What if I never worried about getting rejected again on the phone? What if I took control of the phone call?*

Practicing the next nine steps will change your life. I know because it worked for me...I can't believe I'm thinking this now, but, thank you, Shanell!

STEP 1

You Had Me at Hello

FOLLOWING A SIMPLE PATH THAT NEVER LEADS TO REJECTION

If rejection is one of your biggest fears when picking up the phone, you need a plan that never leads to rejection. If you want a guarantee that you will be embraced by the person on the other end of the call, there is a very simple way.

How? Call your friends. I know, it's almost too easy or good to be true, but it works!

In the professional world, your customers are your friends. These friends—your current client base—can recommend you to prospective customers. About two-thirds of your current customers *want* to recommend you—they just don't know how; they don't know what to say; and they don't think about doing it. Think about the powerful opportunity that exists with nearly six of every ten customers from your current client base. And here's another important piece of info: more than half of all of your clients purchase from you because of YOU. They could buy from anyone, but they buy from you because they like and trust you. There's a tremendous amount of power in that truth that you really need to proactively leverage.

How do you begin to make *that* happen?

Work more aggressively on referrals. Cultivate deeper relationships with your customers. Make sure they know what you do. Make sure they know how to actually articulate what you do to others they know. Help them understand what to say about you. When they have the right words to share your message, help them take the next important step. All you have to do is encourage them. It doesn't have to be a big, awkward formal request. In fact, it should be a no-pressure, gentle reminder. "By the way if you know anybody who needs the special kind of help I provide, let me know!"

A simple "3 BUY 9" strategy can generate warm leads that translate to sales.

Each day, start your day with the same "3 BUY 9" activity. Dial 3 of your current customers, friends or acquaintances by 9 a.m...Get it? "3 BUY 9" is really that simple. What will you say? "Thank you for your business." Follow that up by asking, "What do you like best about doing business with me (or us)?" Follow that up by casually remarking, "Oh yes, one more thing I was going to ask you...do you know anyone who might need my help?" Many customers can't shift mental gears fast enough to think of someone to refer to you immediately. That's okay. They will start thinking. So, say, "I'd appreciate it if you would think about it."

Then what? Typically, my final action on the "3 BUY 9" call is to book an appointment for breakfast the following week to express my gratitude for that customer's business. I mention that I am building a small list of referrals and a collection of recommendations and I hope they can help me out with one of those things, maybe both! Most people are happy to help when they know exactly what you want them to do. The best way for them to know is for you to tell them. The best way to tell them is to keep it unpressured and simple—friend to friend.

The "3 BUY 9" system is all about existing friendships. This kind of call strategy can kick off your day in a very strong way. I've found that starting each day by talking to friends usually puts me in the right frame of mind to cold call potential prospects, the people whom I don't know yet. If you follow the "3 BUY 9" system every day, (remember, many times you land in voicemail) you have a real chance to skip cold calls entirely and start meeting new customers through *warm* calls. Friends of friends are easy to talk to and work with. It's a great way to warm up to making cold calls.

Of course, not everyone will refer you.

So, before you test the "3 BUY 9" approach, let's take a closer look at how things will work so you can understand how to organize your clients in your own mind. There are three categories. The scenario I just described encompasses your largest category: people who know you and like doing business with you. It's about 60 percent of your clients. So what about the other 40 percent? Let's divide those in half to create categories two and three.

Let's take a closer look at each group.

Group One, the largest category, is comprised of people who are willing to refer you, but they simply don't know how. You can change all that by cultivating your relationships with them. Ask them for help!

Group Two is the best category. This is a group of folks I call the true connectors. When it comes to referrals, this is your dream team. They are motivated and inspired to deliver prospects to your door because they are tuned-in to relationships and they like connecting people. Linking people is part of what they do. It's who they are and how they interact in the world.

Group Three has the least potential to help you. It is what I like to call the ole curmudgeon category. It is comprised of people who keep their communication gates locked at all times. These people will not refer or recommend you no matter what the circumstances are. This is who they are and how they interact in the world. They are just wired that way. They believe it is best to keep quiet and they rigidly keep their noses firmly out of everyone else's business—that's how they operate personally and professionally. I might say they don't like to break the rules. I know this group very well because my father is the mayor of this community of people. It's not that Dad doesn't like the service he has received, he just doesn't refer people. Ever. (I still love you, Dad.)

It's important that you have a plan to deal with people like my father. If you don't have a plan, the damage done can be huge. You may wrongly tell yourself, "I ask for referrals but nobody will give them to me."

That's not true.

Remember, two out of every ten people will be like my dad. Eight will not be.

So, here's your plan. When you encounter this sort of individual, recognize what category he or she belongs in. If it's Group Three, accept it. Accept that you will never convince this person to change his mind about referring you. It will not happen. You can't change him. But you can change how you will handle him.

Respond to those who say 'no' by using the follow phrase: "I'm not surprised; however, I will keep working to earn a referral and recommendation from you. I hope that is OK." Pause long enough for them to respond. Be quiet.

Nothing makes people like that more intrigued. At the same time, nothing is more nurturing to your own ego than the graceful mastery of a difficult person and an impossible situation. This reaction safeguards your state of mind and protects your feelings. It helps you recover gracefully from feeling rejected and it allows you to privately acknowledge the real reason for being told 'no'—it's about them, not you. Remember: 20 percent of your client base will not refer anyone to anybody. When you encounter a member of this group, think: I need to direct my time and attention to the other 80 percent who are willing to help me get referrals. I just need to ask for help.

Focusing on the very important people who are most likely to offer referrals to you requires a great plan.

Here's how it works:

The secret to knowing that someone is willing to recommend you is when they send a compliment your way. It could be something very simple. For example, I've had clients say, "Wow, Dave, I love what you've taught me. I really didn't know cold calling could be so easy until you taught me what to do. You really made a difference in my life."

When you receive a compliment, my rule is: return the favor and pass it back. The return compliment would sound something like this: "Thanks! I appreciate that you feel that way. You know, many people who learn new techniques never take action. It makes me feel good that you applied yourself and made things happen. I can't think of a better person to have shared my techniques with!

Now, ask for permission to share how you grow your business. Sharing your story helps deepen the relationship a bit more. I would say something like, "Would it be OK if I share part of my story with you?" Notice, I asked for permission. This step helps weed out the 20 percent who always say 'no' to everything. Remember, you are looking for people who want to engage with you. So, when they give you permission to share an experience, be ready to share a short relevant story from your life. How about something like: "I try to under promise and over deliver my service, so client's like you are willing tell others about how I transformed their business." The goal is to teach them or coach them on how to give you a referral.

Next step: Ask for a referral. You might say, "Perhaps you know someone I could help. Would it be alright if I ask you for a referral?"

If they give you the approval to ask, now is the most important part of the process. You want to teach them what to look for when referring you or your product.

You need to describe your prospects in a way that helps the person choose someone who needs what you sell. You need to paint a very clear picture of what the prospect needs and how you can help. You need to master this strategy not only on the phone but also at networking events and with friends and family before you try it with current clients.

The most difficult part is having enough guts to push a little when a client says, "Let me think about it." It's possible to convince your client to initiate or join you on a three-way call with the person who was referred. It's possible to convince a client to bring the newly referred prospect to lunch to meet you.

Incorporate the "3 BUY 9" strategy into your daily routine as rapidly as possible. Thank clients for their business, ask what you can do better, and last but not least, use the magic words: *do you know anyone else that might use my services?*

When the goal is to 'Have them at Hello', this is how warm leads are generated again and again.

VOICE MAIL TIP

The next time you get voice mail, follow my secret message to success.

"Hey it's me, Dave.
I think it might be important for you to call me back... 772-4909, 772-4909"

then hang up immediately.

Warning: The prospect will call you back. The question is how will you handle the call? Don't be tentative, act like you are expecting a return call.

Make it fun first thing in the morning!

Start each day by dialing 3 BUY 9

Three of your current clients, friends or acquaintances before 9 a.m.

Your script reads like this:

1. Thank you for your business
2. What do you like best about working with me?
3. What can we do better?
4. By the way, do you know anyone who needs my services?

Return any compliment, that's code for they want to refer you.

EXPERIENCE. Share your story about how you grow your business.

ASK. Request a referral and be sure to ask for permission first

MATCH. Yes, match your ideal client for them.

Think **F.A.T.**

I work with people who are:

- Frustrated With? ____________________
  ____
- Aggravated That? ____________________
  ____
- Throw up their arms and quit because?
  ____
  ____

Set your first appointment of the day with a current client to have breakfast and share referrals!

It's a great warm up to the cold call and the first part of "Dialing Strangers."

STEP 2

Who Says It Can't Be Fun and Easy?

A CHECKLIST OF FIVE SIMPLE POINTS THAT WILL GIVE YOU A PASS OR FAIL AFTER EVERY DIAL AND ELIMINATE THE MYTH THAT COLD CALLING HAS TO BE PAINFUL

Ever wonder why cold calling actually works? The truth is so few people actually pick up the phone to prospect that when someone *does* make a genuine effort to dial for an appointment, the odds are they can pretty quickly find success.

No kidding.

Think about that. When it comes to your direct competition in the sales department, you may be one of the only sales professionals who makes a concentrated effort to proactively get the job done. The job, of course, is to fill your sales pipeline with prospective buyers. You cannot book an appointment without talking to someone first.

You may not consciously realize this, but not all buyers are alike.

When you take a close look at the actual sales pipeline, you'll soon discover a few surprises about the types of customers in your pipeline and why making cold calls really does make such a difference about the type of success you can have.

So let's take a look.

Statistics show that in the big sales picture, the types of customers we have to choose from typically fall into three clear categories. It's important to understand these categories, so you can be even more strategic in your effort to make more sales.

The first category is the Dead Zone. About 33 percent of the people out there solidly appear to be potential buyers, when, in fact, they are not going to buy. Think about that. Knowing this dead zone exists is important. It can be hard for many of us to accept this fact, but in many cases—no matter what effort you throw at them—deals with people in the dead zone are not going to happen. So, get ready to let 'em go, or at the very least stop wasting your time working with them.

The second category is the Big Blue Sky Zone. This means that about 33 percent of buyers unexpectedly fall out of the sky to buy from you. That's right. Some prospects are going to buy no matter what...even if the sales person clumsily blunders through the process. You probably can't believe that your efforts might not always matter, but it's true for about 33 percent of the buying public *if you answer the phone or call them back*. Just ask yourself this: have you ever purchased a product even though the sales person was horrible? You know you have. When you made up your mind to buy, nothing stopped you. That's the Big Blue Sky customer. You never know where they are or when they will buy. If you are ready when they are, the sale is yours. So, look to the sky, be on alert and answer the phone. They're the easy ones that will lay down for the sale.

And, then there's the other 33 percent.

The important third category is the Opportunity Zone. Now pay attention. This is where you have the chance to apply your sales techniques and the pay-off will be more sales. About 33 percent of all possible deals waiting out in the world are completely up for grabs. This means that they are waiting for you. All you must do is go out and get your share. If you don't call them, you can't have them. Embracing the **art** of cold calling can change your world.

This is where the fun begins.

When most sales people pick up the phone, they really have no idea what is going to happen. Personally, I used to get scared and my heart rate would pick up. I used to hope that no one would answer the phone on the other end. Then I realized: *what if I make it fun and not focused on me or a sale, but just work on making an appointment?* Now when I pick up the phone, my heart no longer speeds up from fear. If my heart speeds up at all it's from anticipation because now I actually look forward to making the dial. I have a plan and a goal that includes following a script and booking an appointment.

I've discovered while training my methods of Dialing Strangers, that nearly seven out of ten sales people make calls hoping and praying that either the decision maker isn't available or that they get a voice mail greeting. Before you pick up the phone, make sure your mindset is on fun and that what you need for a 'win' is just an appointment. Fun. Appointment. That is all.

It's imperative that you remind yourself that the call is not to 'yell and tell' but rather to relax and dial. Remember to follow the plan. *The worst time to think of what you are going to say is when it comes out of your mouth.*

Practice makes perfect. I remind students all the time that if you are practicing on your clients and prospects, that is called sales *mal*practice. Work on this with family, co-workers and friends. Breathe deep and remind yourself that 'you don't need this sale, you believe in yourself, your company and your product.' Make sure that you are recording yourself. It may sound strange to hear your voice played back to you on speaker; however, that's the only way we can get better. Leave yourself a voice mail, call your office or ask your spouse or significant other to role play with you. Typically, I like to read my script out loud a couple of times to warm up. Remember, the idea of Step One is to get your confidence boosted to the point of not worrying about rejection so much and focusing on fun.

Here's a quick check list as you make your call to see if you are having fun or some form of success. Most managers base success on the sale. I base it on other particular outcomes of the call.

1. **Did I get a Yes?**

   If they want to make a purchase or you sell a one-call product, go ahead and ask for the sale. The best question you can ask is, "Do you want to buy?" (Another great Yes, is getting an appointment.)

2. **Did they give me an unequivocal No?**

   It's true that 'No' is disappointing, but it's a valid answer and it offers an endpoint. Later on, we'll discuss how this can indicate the need to practice. This doesn't mean the process is over, however. For me, it's just the beginning. Love me or hate me; you will never forget me.

3. **This is the fun! Book an appointment.**

   That doesn't mean call me next quarter, swing by in a month, get with me next year. It's defined by actually being put in that person's day planner.

4. **Receive a referral and/or a recommendation.**

   You may not be a fit for them right now, but they may know someone who you can help. You did such a good job with them on the phone, they really do want to help you. (Refer to chapter one for a reminder.)

5. **Learn a valuable lesson from the call**.

   Think about what you need to do better next time. Something that went wrong or didn't happen at all—didn't get a secure date, didn't match personality, or something else. The idea is to improve steadily. Hang up a mirror to remind yourself to smile and have a recorder so you can play back how you sounded after the call and do a quick self-critique. And remember to slow down. It's alright to have quiet space on the phone. Some prospects need space to think. Give them room.

Typically, when I monitor sales people on prospecting calls, they lose the potential client at 'hello.' That is, the client grabs control of the call and the sales person immediately lets go of control. So when the client offers any kind of resistance—like "This is a bad time" or "Call me later" or "I'm busy now" —the sales person will immediately take the off-ramp to Push-Over Canyon. The Push-Over response sounds something like this: "I'm sorry to bother you" or "Yes, I will call next week...What's a good time?" or "No worries...can I call back later today?"

If that's what is happening to you, then here's your chance to step up to the plate. Take a deep breath and find 10 seconds of insane courage. If you are told that it's a bad time then ask, "When would it make sense for me to call back?" "I'm busy now" is followed up with, "That's what I like best about you—you're always busy, like me. Say, what are you busy doing right now?"

Take control of the phone call. If you must call back, get a date and time in their day planner to call back. Please, please, don't take the first time slot they offer up. Pause and say, "Let me look. No, that will not work. How about the following day?" My mission is to make them feel that I'm in such demand they don't want to cancel because I am too hard to make up a date with. Last but not least, when they say I should just call back, follow by saying, "Why on earth would you want me to call back? I assume you'll be busy then." If you make it fun and find the courage to push, you'll be great and, more importantly, cold calling will be fun. Take note, the prospect will notice something different about this call...that it doesn't sound like a sales call at all. That's the mission and you've accomplished it.

Remember:

1. Slow down.
2. If it's a bad time, ask them: "What would be a better time for me to call?"
3. Get in the mindset that you want to relax and have fun with this call.
4. Make a goal to set one new appointment each day. Start at the top and avoid the easy-off ramp or exit.
5. If someone hangs up on you, celebrate with a steak dinner. Trust me, if you follow our system, hang-ups are few and far between.
6. Get good equipment. It helps to have a phone headset and a pocket digital recorder to play back your end of the call and critique yourself. (We are not recommending you record both ends of the call; always follow state rules and regulations.) You can only get better by playing back and listening to your recorded phone conversations.

VOICE MAIL TIP

Did you know that nearly half of the voice mails sales people leave have the word "love" in them?

"I would love to talk with you…"

or maybe it's

"I would love to share with you my new product or idea." And of course "I would love to meet you."

Stop using the word love unless it's referring to your significant other or relative. It's too dangerous of a move. I'll share why later when we study the four personality styles. Tell them you love 'em face-to-face, but never leave a prospect a voice mail with the verb love in it. You can feel the love. Just stop saying "love."

Who says cold calling can't be fun and easy?

Avoiding the biggest failure points before you dial:

- 33 percent of your sales fall out of the sky. Answer the phone, return the message, take the order and enjoy it.
- 33 percent of your leads never happen. Don't focus on nos. Move on.
- 33 percent of the sales pie is up for grabs. Make your fortune here.
- Your single most profitable skill as a sales person is your ability to control the call.
- Get the appointment and remember that practice makes perfect.
- Have a script, mirror, and recorder in front of you at all times.
- The worst time to think of it is when it comes out of your mouth.
- Don't wing it. Practice your script and follow the plan.

STEP 3

Calibrate Your State

HOW TO DEFEAT THE BEAST THAT SAYS, "DON'T TALK TO STRANGERS"

If you hate cold calling, blame your family. That's right. Put the fault exactly where it truly belongs. Mom and Dad. And Grandma and Grandpa, too. You gotta love these people but you need to realize that you learned your dislike for cold calling from somewhere. Most likely, way back when you were a child, your family members told you stuff like, "Don't talk to strangers. Don't take chances." They are the ones behind the big reinforced idea: "Don't ever talk to people about financial issues. Never ask anybody about money."

We all grew up learning this sort of everyday wisdom. The difficult part for you and me now is incredibly clear. As sales people, none of this is true anymore. It's now our job to pick up the phone every day, take a big chance, talk to strangers about financial issues, and, yes, to even ask for money.

You wonder why you detest cold calling? It's a family tradition to hate cold calling!

It's hard to break away from learned behavior. Especially if what you learned is generationally deep. You may even have a family like mine. When I look back at my family history, I am proud of my ancestors, but I also realize it's truly amazing that I ever became successful in my line of work.

The truth is that I had some critical cards stacked against me before I was even born. Quite possibly, when you look at your own roots, you'll find a similar heritage. When I share the following family story, sales people often smile and nod their heads. They usually have an "Aha!" moment about their own lives. So listen in.

In the early 1900s, my great grandparents, Fred and Christine Pearson, were homesteaders on the flatlands of northern Montana. They were determined to teach the value of a dollar to their children and later, to their grandchildren, great grandchildren (that's me), and to their great-great grandchildren (that's my son and daughter). I'm not sure if the phone was even invented when Fred started farming. However, his strong beliefs about money created a legacy that nearly a dozen decades later has directly impacted my cold-calling career.

Before his words of caution ever had a chance to affect me, Fred's belief system first impacted my grandparents. You see, under the watchful eye of Fred my young grandfather, Dave, developed a Ph.D. in farming. Ph.D. back then stood for poor, hungry, and driven. One day, Dave said he was thinking about spending his money on a tractor, but his father-in-law, Fred, warned: "Don't even talk about it. A tractor is too extravagant. People might think you are making more money than you really are. Don't spend money if you don't need to. Save, save, save!"

Now this is where the story gets a bit twisted—it is also the precise point at which some learned behavior originated that I've had to actively reprogram for my own professional success.

Here's what happened. Against Fred's advice, Dave decided to buy the Minneapolis Moline Model 705 diesel tractor. However, before the tractor could actually be purchased, Dave learned to stop talking about money.

So, when he actually bought the tractor he so desperately desired, he was careful not to discuss the issue at all.

How did he manage that?

Simple. Dave stopped talking about money with Fred and with everyone else. And he hid his tractor behind the barn. That's right. He hid the tractor behind the barn so he didn't have to talk about money. Dave had learned: don't ask people about money, or about how much land they farm, or about how many tractors they have. 'Fact is, don't ask anyone anything about finances. No one needs to know.'

My grandfather Dave passed his money beliefs—and those of my great-grandfather Fred–onto his son, our father. Decades later, my father shared the same don't-ask-don't-tell money lessons with my son. In fact, after a day of chores my dad slipped my son a $100 for his hard work, "Don't tell anyone about the money I gave you. No one needs to know", he firmly warned.

You gotta love learned behavior.

But when you recognize the learned behavior is not working for you, you must act to stop it. Know better, do better. As sales people, you and I have to understand the real dynamics at work. Part of understanding others is to first understand ourselves and where our learned behavior comes from. It helps to reflect on the kind of training we received. It helps to recognize that our dear old family may be to blame for our cold-calling fears. And it's nice to try and imagine that the lessons our parents and grandparents tried to share with us were probably the best ones they knew how to offer, even if they were wrong—wrong for us, anyway.

As soon as you can grasp the concept of learned behavior, things can change.

You can change.

How? Take control. One important way to do that is to realize that every person you encounter has learned behaviors from their families, too. We aren't the only ones who inherit old baggage! This is an important realization for many of us. Knowing this allows you to strategically prepare to successfully communicate in ways that your competition will never understand. One way you can succeed is by paying special attention to your tone, tempo, and body language when you make cold calls.

How you look, sound, and pace yourself matters.

Here are some key statistics to understand. About 60 percent of communication is body language. About 33 percent is tone and tempo. The remaining 7 percent of communication is the spoken word. When making cold calls on the phone, you lose nearly two-thirds of communication because you can't see the other person—that is, body language is no longer part of the equation. So, it's critical to focus on tone and tempo. Now that you are on the phone, it accounts for 93 percent of your ability to communicate with the prospect.

With practice, you can learn to tune in to others so you can understand their personalities through their tone, tempo, and choice of words. You can learn to break through communication barriers that may have been established generations ago by their families.

The quicker you can do this, the better.

Most people determine within the first seven seconds of meeting you whether or not they are going to do business with you. So, as a cold-calling sales professional, you need to become very fast at identifying barriers and taking the most successful approaches to really reach an individual and make a strong connection quickly.

As a sales person, you can positively impact your success by learning about the four basic types of people you will routinely encounter. I use the DiSC system to help me calibrate my communication style to match the needs of the people I reach. The DiSC assessment is a behavior evaluation tool based on the theory of psychologist William Marston. Marston's theory centers around four different personality traits: Dominance, Influence, Steadiness, and Conscientiousness– DiSC® Interesting fact: Marston's creation of the test was integral to the invention of the lie detector. The DiSC system isn't meant to find lies; it's meant to uncover truth—as in a person's true nature.

Here's how DiSC works.

When you meet someone new, quickly size them up and decide which personality group is most accurate for who they seem to be. I do this by comparing the individual to a real person I have chosen to represent the DiSC categories in my mind. Here's how I think about people and the DiSC theory when I approach Dialing Strangers:

D stands for Dominant type. Think Donald Trump. This person is decisive, tough, impatient, and strong-willed. Typically, Dominators act quickly and are not usually driven by facts. The Dominator's biggest fear is being taken advantage of. The emotion they typically use is anger, or at least sounding angry. It is often sport for the Dominator to spar with someone on the phone. The secret to the Dominant type is to match the tone immediately. Speak loudly! To Donald Trump, I might say, "Donald, that's what I like about you--you're not afraid to speak your mind. I'm the same way. You're fired!"

TIP: Give this individual fast feedback, stick to one topic and don't slow down their ability to make a decision. The D answers your call, but for some reason is always too busy to talk to you.

I stands for Influencer type. Think Jimmy Fallon from The Tonight Show. Like a great talk show host, this person is sociable, talkative, enthusiastic, and energetic. The Influencer enjoys talking and is very optimistic. The Influencer's biggest fear is not being loved. Notice I didn't say liked; I said loved. I'll coach you on techniques later that stop them from talking so much. However, the secret to the Influencer is to stop, listen, and love.

TIP: Show the Influencer enthusiasm. Smile and make it fun to talk. Do not put them down or focus on details. Use the verb love and always say, "Tell me more." Then sit back, listen and take notes.

S stands for Steady type. Let's think Condoleezza Rice. The former Secretary of State and Stanford professor is a shining example of the Steady at its best. Keep in mind that a third of us fall into the spectrum of the Steady category. So, of all the types out there, this one is particularly important to understand. The Steady is traditionally calm, stable, and laid back. They are caring, patient, and amiable personalities, but they are also stoic and reveal very little emotion. The biggest fear of a Steady personality is **change**. They like things the way they are. The secret to dealing with them is understanding that doing business with you represents change to the Steady. The secret, which can be hard when you're talking on the phone, is to be quiet. Allow the person on the other end of the phone to have time to think. Always offer up a good, better, and best solution. If you asked them to put something on a scale of one to ten, phrase it like this: "I'll give you a minute to think about it. On a scale of one to ten, where do you rate this challenge--ten being great, five being okay, and one being bad?" Give them three choices, time to think about what is correct and also permission to change their mind.

TIP: Do not pressure the Steady, or force them to make sudden changes.

C or Conscientious type. Think of the classic 1950s cop, Sergeant Joe Friday from TV's iconic series Dragnet. Joe's trademark saying was, "Just the facts, ma'am, just the facts." The Conscientious type has a personality that is precise, exact, analytical, and systematic and usually does not express emotions. When it comes to a position that must follow the rules, the C is the ideal candidate for the job. It's important you don't keep information from this person. The C's fear has to do with being criticized or not being "right." When talking to someone on the phone who is a C personality, it's imperative you stick to the facts. Don't criticize the current vendor or product they are using. Don't push too hard because they may go to the angry zone when it comes to emotion. Think about it this way: it's about facts, not feelings, with this particular personality type. Slow down and leave space for them to think when you're talking on the phone. They are careful, disciplined, and precise.

TIP: Do not be chatty with the Conscientious type and don't force them into an immediate decision. Be patient with them. Always give them time to analyze. Remember, they are not interested in having a relationship with you....just the facts.

It's interesting to note that when you are making cold calls, the typical Gatekeeper will often fall under the Influencer or Steady personality type. I've found that the personality of the Gatekeeper usually matches the owner or the manager of the business, but that is not always the case. Remember, the Gatekeeper's job is to let in those who are supposed to see the manager, and keep out those who are not. Match their tone and tempo and discover their personality. When you move past the Gatekeeper or whom I like to refer to as the "director of first impressions," you must then be ready to evaluate the next person and manage their needs, and match personality all over again.

Once you have a sense of how to utilize the DiSC theory, you will probably need to actively focus on transforming another residual learned behavior that can still trip you up. A traditional bit of family wisdom that most of us were commonly taught was The Golden Rule. The Golden Rule says to treat others exactly as you would like others to treat you. In sales, your thought process needs to change from treating people the way you want to be treated to treating people the way their *personality style* says they want to be treated.

That said, it's important to note there is no right or wrong personality types.

Personality types are a lot like shoe sizes. Metaphorically, it's important you know your own shoe size and it helps your career when you can train yourself to figure out the approximate shoe size of others. Chances are you and most of your customers can't comfortably wear the exact same shoes. You don't have to. Like different shoe sizes, it is possible for you to accommodate and understand where people stand in terms of different styles of communication.

Start with yourself.

In terms of personality, metaphorically what size of shoes do you wear? It's time to ask yourself (and whomever might be closest to you): what is *your* DiSC personality type? There are a number of great companies and websites that can provide you with an online or in-person analysis if you want to invest the time and money. Today, though, let's trust your gut.

What are your top two categories?

- **D** = Dominant personality like Donald Trump (like to win)
- **I** = Influencer personality like Jimmy Fallon (love to talk)
- **S** = Steady personality like Condoleezza Rice (want several options)
- **C** = Conscientious personality like Dragnet's Sgt. Joe Friday (like to be precise and right)

As you consider the choices, you may find yourself trying to decide between two different personalities. That's okay. It's normal. In fact, the first personality that comes to your mind is probably indicative of your internal personality. It encompasses the impulses that internally drive you the most. This is the part of you that is likely to represent how you privately think or feel about situations. The second personality is probably the actions or behaviors you shift to when you are under pressure. This is probably how you act or behave out in the world. It's the part of you that others may know and perceive about you. This part of you is how you have learned to behave to be successful in your environment.

Even as you try to figure out your own personality, you may feel like you shift back and forth often between your top two categories. That's normal, too. It's also alright to feel like you have a little bit of each category. For me, my natural personality fits the Dominant slot. Under pressure, out in the world, my personality shifts to Influencer. It's important for me to know that. And, it's important for you to know yourself as well.

All the knowing yourself stuff happens before you ever pick up the phone.

The next step in controlling the cold call is determining the personality of the prospect-the person on the other end of the line. You will need to calibrate your state before your call. Remind yourself what you are. Plan to slow down and match the tone and tempo of the person on the other end. Have your DiSC review sheet handy. Remember not to overreact to their tone and tempo. If someone is loud and short with you, match that tone and tempo. Our goal is to make this fun and fascinating.

Calibrate your state. But, don't start trying this method for the first time on actual cold call prospects. That would not be appropriate. Start by exploring how it feels with people you know and care about. First, figure out yourself. Then, think about friends and family. Then, do some stealth homework on existing clients. Then, and only then, try your hand at cold calling prospects.

Take the time to do the appropriate groundwork and you will never regret it.

VOICE MAIL TIP

When listening to someone's voice mail greeting, determine the personality style by how they word their greeting.

D. "Leave your name and number at the tone." Short, not very sweet, but to-the-point. Your message must be brief. "Call me."

I. Music may play while you're waiting for their voice mail. Listen for the word love as in "I'd love to talk to you, but…." It's usually a message with a lot of talking… . Leave a message stating you'd love a return call.

S. This person follows the rules. The computer voice says, "You've reached the cell phone of…" Then you hear the person's voice say: "David." Then, the computer voice says, "Leave your name and number." That's it.

C. Just the automated operator. That computer greeting voice on your cell phone that says: "You've reached 208-772-4909." No personal greeting of any kind

Take the time to do the appropriate groundwork and you will never regret it.

- D = Dominant personality like Donald Trump (loud, firm)
- I = Influencer personality like Jimmy Fallon (gregarious)
- S = Steady personality like Condoleezza Rice (empathetic)
- C = Conscientious personality like Dragnet's Joe Friday (stoic)

FAMILY AND FRIEND PRACTICE TREE

	Personality type	Biggest fear for that personality	Common things this person says that would support this finding
Mom			
Dad			
Spouse			
Siblings			
Children			
Oldest Friend			
Newest Friend			

Now take this to the next step

CLIENT PRACTICE TREE

	Personality type	Biggest fear for that personality	Common things this person says that would support this finding
Favorite Client			
Oldest Client			
Newest Client			
Past Client			
Other Client			

PROSPECT TREE

	Personality type	Biggest fear for that personality	Common things this person says that would support this finding
Prospect			
Prospect			
Prospect			
Prospect			
Prospect			

HELPFUL HINTS WITH TONE AND TEMPO

Dominant / Donald Trump type(16%)

- Biggest fear is being taken advantage of
- Listen for loud and powerful
- They must win
- Big hearted and benevolent

Influencer / Jimmy Fallon type (41%)

- Biggest fear is not being loved
- Listen for lots of talking
- Enthusiastic

Steady / Condoleezza Rice Type (22%)

- Biggest fear is changing things from the way they are
- Listen for quiet, agreeable and no real opinion
- Offer three choices: good, better and best
- Allow them to change their mind
- Stubborn

Conscientious / Dragnet's Joe Friday Type (21%)

- Biggest fear is being criticized or not being "right"
- Listen for the facts and figures
- Follow the rules
- Details
- Don't leave anything out

STEP 4

Expectations Interrupted

12 WORDS THE GATEKEEPER WILL NEVER SEE COMING

"Hey Dave! Let's play charades—you go first!" Hardly something you would expect someone to say when playing a game of charades. But, you can understand why I did a double take. I was instantly engaged. I realized then that interrupting a person's expectations is a valuable tool for grabbing their attention. The theory is you can control conversations by saying something that is unexpected... people will pay attention to you, tune in, and react. This is one of my key secrets to success on the phone. Expectations interrupted.

So the question then becomes, *how do you interrupt expectations and grab control?*

The secret answer is really not much of a secret at all. To interrupt a listener's expectations, you have to stop sounding like everyone else. My belief is that if your competition is doing it, you need to *stop* doing it. You do not want to start a cold call conversation that follows the same path of every sales person who came before you. "Hi, my name is Dave and I'm calling from AAA Social Media. Who is in charge of SEO for your website?"

Stop meeting the expectations of the listener. Instead, interrupt the expectations of the person who answers the phone.

It's good to be different. It's very good to stand out in a memorable way. If you want to study how to be truly great at interrupting expectations, listen to the best comedians. Standup comics master timing and, more importantly, they excel at making remarks you're not expecting.

Here's one: "I took my wife out to a great dinner for our 25th anniversary. It was a really nice place. It would have been perfect, but I had to back up when we realized they forgot to put ketchup in the bag!" *The punchline is unexpected.*

Here's another: "When asked what I wanted inscribed on my headstone, I told my kids, "Not here yet!"

Okay, I will not quit my day job anytime soon to become a comic, but you are starting to get the idea. Like a comedian, you can say things in a way that surprises people, pushing them to *tune in* and think about what you're saying. If you can make them laugh, you can make them buy, or at least listen. It's not that I want you to be funny. Humor works great, but that is not what I am suggesting you aim for. Instead, I want you to carefully choose the thought path you want to take the listener down and own it. The part I want you to study when watching a great comic is the careful way the comedian crafts the conversation so the audience listens and follows the speaker to the destination of the comic's choice. That is the skill to hone. Like a comic on stage, you can control each and every cold call. You succeed when you say not what people expect, but what they don't expect. Learning how to do this one tiny step at the first instant in the cold call can make a monumental difference in how the entire call unfolds. I've even studied stand-up and how comedians work a crowd by saying the unexpected. You can make this fun by listening closely to comedians or by watching your favorite sitcoms. Take a minute to write down the jokes and think about how the punch line was utilized as a form of expectation interrupted.

It sounds too easy to be true. **But, if you can master how you enter the conversation, you can own it.** That first opening bit can allow you to grab control of the situation. Like a great comic, once you do that, you can find major success and have some real fun.

The best way to start this process is with an easy exercise. I want you to practice my classic cold call opener so much that it becomes a part of your everyday vernacular. Try the following script on your friends and family members until it is second nature to you.

Here are the magic words: "Hey, it's me, (use your name here)...did I catch you at a bad time?" I have generated thousands of appointments and even more money using that phrase!

There is nothing difficult about this opener.

Repeat after me out loud: "Hey it's me, (insert your name)...did I catch you at a bad time?"

This style of greeting needs to be the first phrase you utter when the other person answers the phone. Remember, the phone answerer is not expecting this sort of greeting. You are saying the unexpected. You are interrupting the expectation for phone call protocol. Most sales people who are cold calling will say, "Hello, I'm Dave from ABC Company. Did I catch you at a good time?"

Don't sound like them.

Their type of approach is so common that it's become an unwritten code that actually encourages the listener to shoot them down. This tired approach simply sets off warning bells: "It's a sales person! Go away! It is **never a good time** to talk to someone who is trying to sell me something."

So, don't trigger the alarm system.

Start your call with: "Hey it's me, (insert your name)...Did I catch you at a bad time?"

This greeting will prevent you from sounding like your competition. Let's take a closer look at how my tiny changes to your approach will interrupt the listener's expectations and make results easier to achieve. The first word, "Hey," implies familiarity and even casual friendship without crossing a line. It doesn't misrepresent or trick the listener, it just starts you at a different spot than your competition.

"Hey it's me, (insert your name)..." If you use only your first name, the Gatekeeper or prospect wonders: "*Who is this? Do I know them?*" That uncertainty interrupts their typical flow of thought. They mentally run through their memory file of people with your first name. (Yes, I'm trying to confuse them.) They let their guard down just a little as they try to decide who you are. If you'd said your first and last name and the company you are with, they'd know immediately that they don't know you and their guard then goes up, not down. By interrupting the expectation, you control that opening moment. For an instant, your listener is wondering how to respond. That instant of uncertainty allows you to take another step.

Don't waste time. Continue with the script. "Did I catch you at a bad time?"

The automatic reflex for most people is to say: "No." (This question or statement is my form of a secret lie detector test. Whatever they say is probably true.)

Most people say no more often than yes, without even thinking. That's what makes your new script so beneficial to you. The expected question is "Did I catch you at a good time?"

By interrupting the expectation, **you control that opening moment**.

You will say it in an unexpected way: "Did I catch you at a bad time?"

By changing the question around, the typical 'no' response is now a good response for you. Obviously, if it really is a bad time, they will tell you that on the spot. But, typically it's not an automatic turn-down. It is usually after they stop, think about it, and really consider the question you have asked. If they say it is a bad time, your answer is: "OK, when would it make sense for me to call you back?"

But, let's not go too far in that direction yet.

The focus of this chapter is to get the cold call off the ground in the right way and on the right trajectory. That takes practice. So, practice the new opening script at least ten times on friends and family members.

I mean it. Don't practice on clients and prospects. (More on that in a moment.)

Please make that call to one family member or friend right now. Take action so we can move on to controlling the rest of the call. Becoming comfortable with the opener takes some time and patience. You want to practice on friends and family so that you can become good at your new routine. As you try this opener, listen to how your tone of voice sounds with the people you know. Be ready to duplicate that tone and timing with strangers.

When it's time to start cold calling, you must have faith in yourself to pull it off. If you don't believe first in yourself, second in your product, and then in your company, please do not pick up the phone and dial. You must genuinely believe you have the potential to help your prospects, or you shouldn't be calling on them.

Learn to tell yourself: these people are waiting for me to call and change their business.

"Hey, it's me, (use your name here)...did I catch you at a bad time?"

VOICE MAIL TIP

Over half of the people I train have a secret wish when making a cold call. When we first start the process, they secretly hope and pray they get voice mail and not a real live person. The idea is they can tell their manager that they made the call and left a message, pretending to do the sales job of calling. At the same time, they don't actually have to worry about selling anything. Here's my suggestion: listen to voice mails very carefully and leave a message that makes sense to their personality style.

If the voice mail opens with automation followed with their own voice saying, "David Jon," then ends with the automated voice: "is not by the phone now," this is a Steady personality. Give them three times that would work best to call you back. For example, "Call me back at noon, 4 p.m. or first thing tomorrow morning at 8 a.m."

If they speak loudly and quickly and say something like, "At the tone, you know what to do," or if they tell you, "Send an email or text," this person is more than likely a Dominant personality. Remember to speak up and state what's in it for them right away. Keep your message short.

If the voice mail states the day, date, and when they return calls and when they are in and out of the office, mirror the message. Be very specific with no emotion or tone. *Just the facts* and no feelings will grab their attention. This person is more than likely a compliant, or Conscientious, personality.

TAKE ACTION RIGHT NOW!

What exactly is meant by Expectations Interrupted? Saying something other people don't expect, similar to a punch line in a joke.

If your competitor is doing it, stop doing it. (Find out. Call and see how they answer the phone.)

The prospect answered the phone, now what should I do?

Practice a simple phrase with friends and family: "Hey, it's me, (use your name here)... did I catch you at a bad time?"

STEP 5

Getting Past the Gatekeeper

A HELPING HAND FROM THE GATEKEEPER IS ALL YOU NEED

Asking the Gatekeeper to give you a hand into the front door: *The secret to getting the person at the front desk to invite you into the corner office.*

Fear begins at the front desk. Not just for you. For all of us. That's because each company's front desk is strictly guarded by a Gatekeeper. In your mind's eye, when you visualize that Gatekeeper, your imagination may conjure up some mean monster akin to Nurse Ratched from the classic film, *One Flew over the Cuckoo's Nest* starring Jack Nicholson.

Talk about scary.

No wonder you feel fear when you prepare to cold call. There's only one thing to do. Let's face your worst fear and see what part is true and what part is imagined. Separating the true parts from the imagined parts changes everything. So let's get going.

It's true that every place you call has a Gatekeeper.

However, it's not true that every Gatekeeper is the same. It's also not true that most Gatekeepers are mean. In reality, most business owners want to hire a Gatekeeper who exudes friendliness. That friendliness can make up for what the company may lack in the public relations department. For some companies, that Gatekeeper personally represents an ideal vision of happiness that the boss wants to project—the happy boss / happy company vision. This is important to know as you deliberately try to replace preconceived notions of Gatekeepers with more accurate understandings.

Next truth?

It's true that half of the Gatekeeper's job is to let in those who are allowed to talk to the decision maker. That means friends, family, clients, and usually prospects who want to buy that company's product or service can pass quickly through the gates. You may imagine that the Gatekeeper knows all these people personally. The truth is he/she knows some, but not all. Because Gatekeepers don't know them all, they make some general assumptions about people who approach the gates. They let in the ones they know. And they let in the ones they think they probably should know. This is important to consider as you try to figure out ways to get past the Gatekeeper. You need to ask yourself how friends, family and clients talk to each other and what that may look like to the Gatekeeper when a decision is being made about whom to let in and whom to keep out.

Why is this important? Because every day you must get past multiple Gatekeepers to survive in your work role.

Next truth? The other half of the job for the front desk Gatekeeper is literally to stop strangers from reaching the decision maker. And, yes, "strangers" is really code for sales people like you and me. So, in reality, at least half of the Gatekeeper's job is to stop you from doing your job. Until now, you may have only imagined that might be true—well, it is.

It's absolutely true that every Gatekeeper you meet has been instructed to stop sales calls from reaching the manager, owner, or other decision makers. You may imagine that the Gatekeeper is a natural Nurse Ratched 24/7, but the truth is that your "salesman" talk ignites a Gatekeeper response that mimics the cranky version of Nurse Ratched. Any form of, "My name is Dave and I'm calling from the office of Dialing Strangers, which by the way is the best cold call training anywhere in America. Can you tell me who's in charge at your office?" will be met with, "She's not in, but I can take a message and have her call you back." If you imagined that response is really code for "Thanks, but no thanks," you are right. If you're lucky, your call will be noted with a Post-it note in the decision maker's mail box; however, most of the time, you will never get past the junk mail pile or the recycle bin.

So, now that you've faced some hard truths, what can you do?

Take the tools we have discussed in the previous chapters, and make those tools work for you. Here and now. Together at once.

Remember DiSC? Well, it's important that you have your tone and tempo chart close by to consider the DiSC personality type when you encounter the Gatekeeper. Most Gatekeepers are going to fall under the category of Influencer or Steady personality. Keep in mind those two types are very close together. That means a Gatekeeper may swing under pressure from S to I or vice versa very easily.

Now think about Expectations Interrupted. By now, you've practiced and mastered the surprise approach. So, your next step is to specifically apply that concept to the Gatekeeper. Remember, you must get past the Gatekeeper to do your job. The Gatekeeper's job is to stop you. Your job is to get through the gate. It's a game of strategy. You must get through the gate because the decision maker needs what you are selling. If you do not believe that, stop now. If you do believe it, find a way through the gate.

Next truth? The Gatekeeper might let you through the gate if you are strategic about how you handle yourself.

One of the most enduring wartime tales deals with getting past the Gatekeeper. That story details how the Greeks entered the city of Troy during the Trojan War by outsmarting the Gatekeepers. The battle was said to rage on for over a decade until the Greeks came up with a plan to get into the city and past the great walls. Their plan consisted of leaving a giant wooden horse on wheels at the gates of Troy. The beautiful horse appeared to be a gift, presumably a war trophy, to the residents of Troy. The Gatekeepers opened the gates and let the great equine carving enter the premises. Late at night, a group of Greek soldiers who were hidden inside the great carving, lowered themselves from the Trojan horse into the city of Troy and opened the gates for the other Greek soldiers to enter, claim victory, and ultimately end the war.

The Trojan Horse technique is an interesting concept for you. You aren't really at war and you don't want to misrepresent yourself or cause any harm to any Gatekeepers or their companies. But you *do* want to get past the gates. You can be as strategic as the Greeks and allow the Gatekeepers to jump to their own conclusions and act upon them.

The best Trojan Horse technique for you is needing help.

You're lost and you need some help. (Fact: 99 percent of us want to help people in need.)

The Gatekeeper will want to help you when you're lost.

Allow yourself to be rescued.

I say, "I'm a little lost here. I'm wondering if you can help me." You will be greeted by silence. Don't say anything until the person on the other end answers with help. My request becomes the vehicle to get me in the door and it ends the potential battle between me and the Gatekeeper before it even starts. Along with being a little lost, I will also add, "I'm not even sure if I should be calling or talking to you." That admission typically makes Gatekeepers swing the door wide open and offer not only to help me themselves, but also to offer to connect me to someone farther up the ladder who can help. Most Gatekeepers ask me what part of the city and what street I'm on when I ask for directions.

When I utilize the Trojan Horse technique, two great things happen. The Gatekeeper is ready and willing to help me and now the mind is off being the Gatekeeper and shifts to letting me in.

To do this well, Expectation Interrupted and Trojan Horse techniques must go hand and hand and without a pause. The idea is to deflect the gate keeper's radar of who should go in the front door and who should be kept out.

No matter how cynical we become, it's imperative to remember that our natural instinct is to help people. The inner self is wired to help a fellow human with a flat tire, looking for directions, or in need of a hand.

So, think about how you can make this work for you.

The first secret to the Trojan Horse technique is to ask for help. It sounds something like this. "I'm a little lost here; I'm wondering if you can help me ?" It's imperative that you practice that line with tone and tempo, pausing just past the "I'm a little lost here" and holding out the word "wondering" in the second half of the statement, "if you can help me out?"

Emphasize the question mark after you say the word "out." I'm told by those that take my one-on-one and day-long cold call I sessions that before they started the program, they worry they'd sound too scripted.

The secret is to *own* your script. It's not the size of your part, but what you put into it that matters. Focus on your part.

Remember: a big part of what you are doing is orchestrating a little Gatekeeper **confusion.** That's part of doing your job. If you are struggling right now with ethics or worry that you're misleading someone, ask yourself whether the decision maker needs what you are selling. (Remember: If you don't believe first and foremost in yourself then the product, and finally your company, you shouldn't be calling.) If you do believe that someone is waiting for you help on the other side of the gate, do what you can to gain access to them and offer the help they need.

The secret is to practice this technique. Don't try it on an actual prospect. Instead, practice by calling a friend's business. My dad is a veterinarian and I practice whenever I call his office. You would think by now they'd know my number, but it works like a charm. "Hey it's me Dave, did I catch you at a bad time?"

"No, sir."

"I'm a little lost here, I'm wondering if you can help me?"

"I'll try."

"I'm not even sure if I should be talking to you, but Doc said to call him here. Can you put him on please?"

"Let me see......can I tell him who is calling?"

"Sure, it's me, Dave!" Go silent. Practice makes perfect and this is how the person at the front desk can get you to the backroom. Here's why this works: because only someone calling and asking for "Doc" would be the doctor's personal friend or family member. They are the only ones that are allowed to call him that, right?

VOICE MAIL TIP

In small business environments, nearly 80 percent of the Gatekeepers I survey have a personality style similar to the owner or the decision maker in the company. Most of us buy from people or hire people who are like us. So, if the owner of the company is very outgoing and wants customers and prospects to be treated a certain way on the phone, more than likely the Gatekeeper will have that same personality. Usually, they are the I of the DiSC. That means when you're speaking with them on the phone or trying to move up the ladder to the next person in line, use the verb 'love' and build some form of bonding and rapport. Remember, however, if the owner is a rule follower, or a classic technician type of owner, the Gatekeeper may mirror that. In that case, don't talk to him about feelings, stick to the facts and offer up choices of a return call time and don't keep anything from him. This doesn't always work, but as you're doing your detective work in building a case to make the sale, keep in mind there is an eight out of ten chance that the Gatekeeper's tone and tempo will match that of the owner or decision maker.

TAKE ACTION RIGHT NOW!

Ask the Gatekeeper to help you get in the front door and back to the corner office.

- A Gatekeeper's job is to let in friends and family and others who are supposed to come in
- The gatekeeper will keep out those who are not allowed in – like sales people
- Your mission is to confuse the Gatekeeper. Make them think they had better let you in because you might be someone important and they don't want to get in trouble
- Also remember 99 percent of people including the Gatekeeper will want to help you
- Own this phrase and practice on family and friends all the time: "I'm a little lost here...I'm wondering if you can help me?"

STEP 6

"No" Just Means Practice

IT'S OVER WHEN WE SAY IT'S OVER, NOT WHEN THE PROSPECT SAYS IT!

One of my cold call trainees calls it the "Click of Shame." Interestingly enough, when I hold live cold call training and I ask the entire team to make outgoing cold calls, on average it takes nearly 50 minutes or longer for someone to get hung up on. They are all trying to get the "Click of Shame" because I offer a big prize for the first hang up. Here's my point: we fear being rejected, but most prospects don't hang up.

"NO!" We hate the sound of it. We hate the feel of it.

As small children, NO is a seriously defeating end to an experience we had hoped with all our hearts would turn out differently. As adults, NO is even worse. Sometimes, we hear NO before anyone actually says it. Remember my sixth-grade crush on Shanell? Remember when she picked up the phone and said hello to me? I hung up the phone before I spoke to her because I was filled with fear. She never actually told me NO. She didn't have the chance because I imagined a negative outcome and disconnected. If I had maintained the courage to see my initial quest to its true end, I would have likely discovered that this girl was flattered by my call. Instead, what I learned from that cold call was that it's over when I say it's over…and it's important to never let fear of rejection end the call before it even has a chance to begin. You may do that, too. Stop. Think about that. You need to actually make the ask. You need to allow the person time to respond.

You may hear YES.

Of course, you may hear NO.

After the Shanell incident, I eventually called other girls and asked them out. Some of those girls said NO. What I learned from those subsequent personal cold calls became important in my professional life. I learned firsthand that NO won't kill you. In fact, it can help you.

I also learned I was able to acquire more YES responses when I took the time to rethink NO.

I realized I hated to hear NO because when someone said NO I imagined they were really saying FAILURE. NO does not mean FAILURE. NO really means GO PRACTICE.

To be truly successful at anything, **practice is required**. My motto is, "The worst time to think of it is when it has already come out of your mouth!" The truth is that you will fail sometimes. Failure isn't being told NO. Failure is hearing NO and allowing that to stop you from trying at all. NO does not mean QUIT. NO means PRACTICE. Failing means success is ahead. It seems counterintuitive, but it's true. To achieve success, you must experience failure along the way. Legendary sales trainer Tom Hopkins liked to say that we're not judged by the number of failures, but by how many times we succeed.

So, failure happens....and it happens on the road to success. NO is the reminder for you to practice. Let me add one more caveat to the call. It's over when I say it's over. Repeat that out loud to yourself right now.

Let NO inspire you to try again.

Cold calling is like learning to ride a horse. The first time I was bucked off a horse on my grandparents' ranch in

Montana, I was told to get back in the saddle. Learning to ride a horse means you have to get back on. Likewise, when someone tells you NO on the phone, it's time to practice.

So, how do you practice?

Learn your script. Discover what to say and how to say it. Have a clear purpose and plan in mind when you make each call. And, always remember that the call is not over until you say it's over—you're in charge of every call. If you're told NO, it means PRACTICE.

It may seem simple, but the techniques I've been sharing with you work. And my cold call methods work so well, that I am routinely willing to put my money where my mouth is. When I teach cold call camps, I put the techniques we've been discussing in this book to the test in real time in front of a training audience filled with sales professionals. It's exciting and fun for me now, but the very first time I decided to prove that NO means PRACTICE, it was a little terrifying. If you think you're nervous picking up the phone alone to make a cold call, imagine doing it on stage on a speaker phone in front of a bunch of cynical pharmaceutical sales representatives.

That group all but begged me to prove that my techniques would work in their arena. I decided that seeing—no, better yet, hearing—was believing. So, I put a speaker phone on stage. Now, to fully understand the situation, you have to know a little bit about the sales environment for a typical pharmaceutical rep. To put it mildly, it's a brutal world out there for them. The job of a pharmaceutical rep often consists of going into a doctor's waiting room with coffee and sandwiches on the required day of the week and hoping and praying the doctor will think you are good enough and worthy enough to share five minutes of time to talk to you about your product—the latest, greatest prescription drug on the market.

That's what it's like face-to-face. Imagine the thought of calling a medical office in a cold call setting and asking to get through to the doctor. Remember the Gatekeeper?

Asking that crowd to apply my techniques was counter-intuitive to them. Everyone likes to think they're the exception to the rule.

My cold call approach seemed to break every unwritten rule in the pharmacy reps' version of Robert's Rules of Order on what you can and cannot do when booking an appointment with a doctor. The entire room was terrified when I picked up the phone and dialed a doctor's office to prove my methods work. I was a bit terrified myself because this industry was outside of my own industry experience. But it's how I came to confirm my approach works no matter what industry you're in.

Here is how the call played out.

I knew the secret to success was not to sound like every other sales rep who called. How could I be different from the others? I recalled that most of my dad's close friends and family call him by the nickname Doc. He's a veterinarian. Looking back now I realize that Doc is a sort of accepted code the inner circle uses and to others it simply means, "I know him and he's a friend of mine."

When the hospital receptionist answered my call with her routine greeting, I responded in a familiar tone, "Hi Karen. It's me, Dave. Did I catch you at a bad time?"

"No. It's not." When Karen followed my script, I saw a room full of mouths drop wide open. The sales reps couldn't believe it. So far, so good.

I responded quickly, "Is Doc in?"

Man, oh man. If you could have seen the wave of shock register on the faces of those in my training audience. The picture was priceless. The sales reps looked like they were thinking that the AMA was going to bust down my door and arrest me for acting so casual to a doctor's receptionist.

On the phone, the receptionist paused. Then she said, "Who would you like to talk to?"

I said, "Doc, of course. Tell him it's me, Dave!"

The vibe of my training room spiked with nervous tension. The sales people leaned forward as if on command. We all listened as the receptionist covered the phone. We could hear her muffled voice asking the doctor if he knew me. We could hear him affirm that he knew a Dave. Which one was I? She came back on the line. "Do you mean Dr. Nelson?"

I responded, "Of course. Put him on."

"Will he know who you are?" She continued doing a great job as the Gatekeeper.

"Tell him it's me—Dave. I can wait."

Guess who came on the phone? Dr. Nelson. And, no, he didn't hang up on me. Part of the process is having a plan and knowing where to go with it. I shared my info in an upbeat, positive way and he accepted that I was worthy of his time. Of course, the bottom line was that I was worthy of his time. And you are too, if you believe in yourself and what you're offering.

So, what happened? As we talked, it became clear that he wasn't a good fit for the product I was trying to tell him about. But, reaching that conclusion did not mean the call was over.

NO does not mean NO.

After we'd established that we were not a match, it was time for me to practice.

NO means PRACTICE. I said, "Dr. Nelson, it sounds like I'm not a fit for your needs. Would you by chance know anyone else whom I could help?"

Most of us, myself included, could have stopped at hello. The receptionist was a decent Gatekeeper and calling a doctor is potentially confidence-shattering. When I eventually heard NO, I could have politely hung up and quickly apologized for wasting his time. However, it's important for you to push ahead and take out that head trash that says you're not worthy to make the call...that they don't want what you have, and that NO means NO.

Remember, NO means PRACTICE. But more importantly, it means the call is over when I say it's over. That's not a case of braggadocio. It's used to protect my head and keep the Shanell Incident at bay.

When I asked for a referral, the doctor gave me one. Quite simply, he knew that my goal was to find people I could help. He believed that about me and he was willing to help me, help others.

After the referral, I was still not done with the call. "Say, Doctor, my sense is I didn't do a very good job on this call to you. What can I do better next time I make a call to an MD's office like yours?"

By rethinking NO, I was encouraged to allow that call to help me become a better sales person. You can, too.

After this demonstration, a pharmaceutical rep said something I will never forget. This rep was the guy who was sure that doctors would never talk to sales people on the phone. When we proved his theory was wrong, he turned to the entire class and said, "Dave, you've got more guts than anyone I've ever met in my life." Well, that is not what is required. Remember, when someone says, "NO," it really means practice. The call is over when you say it's over. So go out and be bold by practicing your craft.

VOICE MAIL TIP

I hate to be that guy who says, "I thought everyone knew this." I know everyone doesn't know this tip, so here it is...

When I get the automated operator while asking to speak to the decision maker, nine times out of ten, I'll touch zero on my phone. It will ring to a live person, whom I've found is typically not the Gatekeeper, but instead the in-house operator.

If I'm trying to contact a decision maker named Jim Parker, the call goes like this. No matter who answers, say, "Jim is that you?" The operator will say, "No... excuse me?" Then, I become a great actor. "I was just talking to Jim and I got cut off, please page him!" I have no idea if they have a paging system, however, if they do, Jim will answer and if they don't, the operator will do everything in his or her power to connect me to the decision maker I asked for. It starts by touching zero and never settling for voice mail!

TAKE ACTION RIGHT NOW!

The worst time to think of it is when it comes out of your mouth!

"NO!" Just Means Practice: SO, have a practice plan in place and roll with the punches.

The call is over when we say it's over. Repeat this out loud please! Along those lines, remember you can't lose anything that you don't have, so stop worrying about what others are thinking. Here are some remarks that will serve you well...practice saying them. Also, extend the call one more question than you feel comfortable doing. I promise it will only hurt for a little bit.

- I thought you might say that. I don't suppose you know anyone else who...?

- I get the feeling I've upset you. What could I have done better on this call?
- Do you know anyone else in your office or line of work who might be interested in my service?
- Oh, real quick before you go, let's pretend you were interested in our product…what would you be looking for?

STEP 7

Magic Script

WORDS THAT WILL MAKE YOU RICH

These words are very valuable tools. In fact, the right words can make you rich.

Got your attention?

We're about to figure out what sequence of words you need to string together to help people understand who you are and what you do...and to help them *want* to buy what you are selling.

What are the right words for you?

Think about this--if I were to recommend you to a potential customer, what would I tell them about you or your business? The words you come up with right now could cause a sale to happen very quickly. The words you tell me to say could open the financial flood gates in ways that you never even imagined possible.

So, what words are the right words for you?

When I ask that question to a group of trainees, many people have no clear answer. Or they choose a group of worn-out words or tired phrases that sound like I might be talking about almost anyone. Sometimes I hear, "Tell them that we've been in business for a long time." Other times I am told, "Say that we are honest and ethical." Often, I am given the blanket instruction, "Tell them we do what we say we're going to do."

Really?

Well, let's cut to the chase right here. Dull, boring words are not good enough for you to use to represent yourself. Furthermore, stale, trite phrases are not good enough for me to share. My goal is to drum up serious business. That should also be your goal. The right words can make that goal happen.

So why aren't you using the right words? Probably because the right words are not the easiest words to find. Many businesses make a big mistake while formulating a marketing plan. They may adore their name or get hooked on something they noticed on a road-side sign and opt for that as a catch phrase. The real challenge for many modern companies is that they simply can't effectively communicate *why* they are in business. Often when they try to speak up, they talk about why they are doing things, instead of focusing on the details that the clients or prospects really care about.

Think about that. They choose the wrong words. They don't think about what the customer really needs to know. So, answer the same question now: If I were to recommend you to a potential customer, what would I tell them about you or your business?

If you want to find the very best answer to that question, call your top ten customers. When you call them, ask them this simple question, "Why do you buy from me?"

As you hear what they say, listen. Really listen. You need to do more of what they are talking about. And you need to help others understand what your real customers actually like about you. Take notes when your customers tell you why they buy from you.

These are the words that can help make you rich.

This is the point in the process where my Magic Script comes into the big picture. You need a script to teach a prospective customer about your business and why your company can be the solution. An important thing to remember is that marketing is similar to teaching. The best way to practice creating, editing, and delivering your Magic Script is at networking events when other business owners or sales people come up and ask what you do or what service you provide. Tell them what your customers told you. Actively transform that bunch of customer comments into a Magic Script that will work for you.

How?

I have a formula for that. All you need to do is plug in the unique details from your notes. Here is the opener for your Magic Script: "I help A understand B so they can C." Here is the key:

- **A** = who
- **B** = what
- **C** = get these benefits and results

Here are two examples of Big Openers: "I help small business owners understand marketing and sales so they can generate new leads and close sales." "I help horse owners understand riding techniques so they can participate in rodeos without spending a lifetime in the saddle."

After you open, you need to follow up with a special set of examples.

These examples are called the Big Three Aches and they're part of your Magic Script. I have a formula for this part, too. (I like formulas!) You need to work hard so that each line is tailored to *your* situation and sounds natural on the phone. In each instance, finish the line with your own details and replace the word 'people' with something more specific, if possible.

Line number one: For example, I work with (people) who are aggravated about....

Line number two: I also work with (people) who are frustrated about....

Line number three: I work with (people) who are ready to throw up their hands....

Here is an example of my entire Magic Script. You will note that in some instances, I moved the phrases around a little to tailor the sentences to my natural manner of speaking.

The Big Opener: "I help sales people who are asked to generate leads on the phone. I have a proven system from dial to appointment that will help them create more dollars and value for their life and clients than ever before."

The Big Three Pains: "For example, I work with sales people who are aggravated after being told they would be trained on the art of cold calling, only to get a 'go get 'em kid' and a three-year-old call list. And I work with sales managers who are frustrated that after a handful of rejections, their sales team stops dialing and starts complaining that the leads and products are simply no good. I also help entrepreneurs and business owners who are so concerned with the lack of a cold calling process that works, they are ready to throw up their hands and sell the business."

You can fill in the blanks for your business, but the key here is to paint a vivid picture with real details that will resonate with your listener. Clear descriptions allow the prospect to feel like you are an advisor rather than a phone solicitor. The idea of the Magic Script is to help you stand out from your competitor.

It may not feel comfortable at first following the Magic Script. However, to paraphrase Donald Trump, in order to achieve, you must feel uncomfortable 75 percent of the time. This script will not feel normal or comfortable when you first start using my process. The key, however, is to practice over and over again, so it becomes second nature.

Then, it's like having a commercial that really works. People will respond to you when you set the stage. Once you set the stage, you say something like, "I don't suppose you are suffering from any of these issues or know anyone in your company who is?"

VOICE MAIL TIP

My wife isn't a big fan of me doing this (or coaching you to take action on this technique) but it works. She doesn't like it because it's breaking the rules of calling. When I struggle getting someone to answer and find myself on voice mail leaving a message that won't be returned, I change my time to call. I make dials early in the morning, 7 a.m., and start experimenting with the automated operator. Typically, pound or # T works when I'm trying to track someone down. It usually tells the phone system this is a transfer call. From that point, I work to the automated phone book. You can dial after 5 p.m. or late at night and on weekends. That's the part my wife doesn't like. She wonders, "What if you are interrupting or calling them when they are working on a big project?" That's the point!

Warning: Never use any of my tips unless you believe in yourself. Believe in your product and believe in your company.

TAKE ACTION RIGHT NOW!

Our Magic Script can make you rich.

(I help A understand B so they can C)

- **A** = who
- **B** = what
- **C** = get benefits and results

OR

We are a ______________________
company that helps ______________________
understand ______________________

I help (people) who are aggravated with
____

We help (people) who are frustrated with
____

We also assist (people) who are ready to throw up their hands and __________________ the business because of _____________________________________

Work on this script and master it. I usually suggest to most of my clients that they create a handful of scripts (at least three or four) to have an appropriate repertoire for different products and services you might handle. Not all prospects are equal or have the same pains. One prescription will not cure all ailments unless you are selling snake oil.

STEP 8

Agonizer Sequence

POWERFUL PAIN QUESTIONS THAT WILL HAVE THEM DIALING 911

After a weekend of working in the garden in early spring, you might wake up with a very sore back on the following Monday. You aren't afraid of the pain because you know what caused it. The soreness may be significant and it may be a nuisance, but you don't even think about visiting a doctor because the pain isn't that bad. You feel achy and agitated about being slowed down, but you know this sort of thing happens. You tell yourself that you don't need anyone to help you because you know from past experience that a couple of Ibuprofen will resolve the discomfort.

Most people in business operate in a similar fashion. When they encounter a hard day, they do what they can to muddle through it.

But, what if you play a different scenario through your mind?

How would you feel about the same situation if you woke up the following Monday in the same significant pain and there was no direct explanation for the hurting? If the pain was bad enough, you might feel a wave of fear wash over you. You might have an epiphany that you really have been in pain for a while and for some reason you blamed that pain on things that weren't really causing it. That realization might cause a wave of panic that forces you to wonder what might happen next. You might flash for an instant on a mental image of yourself in a wheel chair. If the pain was bad enough or the fear was large enough, you probably would feel compelled to book an appointment to see a doctor later in the week. If the pain was severe enough or your fear about the pain was strong enough, you might even call 911 for immediate help.

Most people in business operate like this, too. They ignore the aches and pains if they can and they don't do something about the agony until they realize things are really dire. Understanding this dynamic is critical. Taking ownership over your role in it will make you a successful sales person.

So what do you need to know?

Typically, only 20 percent of purchase decisions are based on the desire to gain something or on the desire for immediate satisfaction. And the price of the purchase plays a large role in that. The real decision to purchase a product comes from a place of agony. Nearly 40 percent of why people buy is based on fear. In the case of a bad back, fear is not being able to walk again. The other 40 percent of why people buy comes from agitated pain or the potential of what could happen if they don't get a broken bone cast, for example. There is a difference between simple pain and agitated pain. Simple pain is the actual soreness. Agitated pain is when a person wants to do something but the pain is a barrier. For example, the individual wants to go to work but the pain won't allow the movement needed to get in the car. A person in agitated pain will typically feel compelled to do something to resolve the issue that stops him or her from doing a desired activity.

Fear and pain are great motivators for humans to take action. That's the real reason why most people buy from you. Knowing this one important fact means you can leverage this truth to help you succeed. So, start leveraging.

Your role is to help prospects find their way through the agony of business. How can you help? Listen to them. The key to listening is asking great questions. You need to rapidly determine exactly what kind of pain each person is in so that you can provide the solution that will help immediately.

Most sales people don't ask the kinds of questions that can get the responses you're looking to get. In fact, I've found the natural question most sales people like to ask is very general. Most sales people approach the client with a general question about the business and a follow-up inquiring what the biggest challenge might be. The reality is that an approach like that is very amateur. Most business owners or prospects don't have time to teach you about their business and they usually don't trust you enough to break out the deep, dark secrets of why they are struggling. To lower that defensive sales guardrail, and at the same time keep yourself from talking too much, it helps to have a plan.

So, let's focus on what that plan needs to look like.

Remember, we start with the Magic Script. Remember how we crafted your Magic Script around the Big Opener: "If I were to recommend you or your company to someone, what would I tell them about your product?" Then, we build a set of Three Big Pains tailored around your typical client base.

If you have targeted your prospects, this type of Magic Script sets the stage for the Agonizer Sequence.

The Agonizer Sequence is all about defining and understanding the prospect's pain.

I like to ask precise questions that will really help customers identify and define their genuine needs. The mere act of asking questions they have never been asked before moves us into a new, deeper relationship. Showing interest and asking meaningful questions transforms me from ordinary sales guy to business counselor or, at least, from ordinary sales guy to someone who is obviously practiced and seasoned in the trade.

I start with the question: "Let's pretend you and I were to meet up or talk on the phone one year from right now. What would have had to have happened for you to be pleased with your progress?"

When asked this unusual question, which they have likely never been asked before, something surprising happens with business people. Most prospects provide a meaningful answer. The answer that pops out is usually delivered with some excitement. It's almost like the info has been locked inside, waiting to spring out of them. I write what they are saying on a white board in big bold letters for all to see I'm trying to help them discover and pinpoint their real issues. And, more importantly I'm giving them some room to think about the bigger picture. One year from today broadens the scope and changes how they feel. It puts the future into the present.

The Agonizer Sequence is all about understanding and even almost feeling the agony they feel.

I'm not going to ask them to buy or make a decision right now. My goal is to turn the sales pressure off. I am turning the pressure off of me and, more importantly, I am turning the sales pressure off of the prospect so he or she can discover what the problem is and decide if meeting face-to-face with me makes sense.

Let's take a look at what this scenario might look like in the field.

Let's say your prospect is a man who owns a bank. He says he would be pleased if his account managers would start cross-selling other banking services to every new client who walks through the door to open a checking account.

Fair warning.

When he tells you this initial issue, remember, this is probably not the real deep-down challenge he is facing. Don't try to fix the initial problem without a sales X-ray first.

Just listen and ask the next question. That next question sounds something like this: “Maybe you could give me a recent example of this happening for you and your team.” This allows the prospect to go deeper into the issue. Going deeper helps pinpoint the problems with real clarity.

Next, I use what is called the zero technique of questioning which can have me repeat the last couple of words they said. After they make the statement about opening a checking account. I say, “...when opening a checking account?” which again has them going deeper without me saying, “Tell me more!”

Now, as this occurs, the key is not only to have a yellow pad and pen in front of you, but to also take copious notes. The notes will be useful later because 90 percent of what you don’t write down, you will forget. You need notes to remember everything.

Before you take notes, always ask if it’s okay to take notes. That’s like secretly telling them that I’m intently listening to what they are saying.

I tell the person on the other end of the phone that they may hear me typing on my keyboard or taking some longer than normal pauses. I make a point of explaining that this doesn’t mean I’m not listening or that I’m not paying attention. It means that I'm making sure I'm noting and listening to everything they are saying so I don't forget...and I ask if that is okay. This simple step shows respect and puts me in the driver's seat in terms of controlling the cold call.

The mission—especially here—is to be a great listener.

I need to know what they want to do. I need to ask: "What have you tried or what are you currently doing to get your tellers to cross-sell and upsell new members at your bank?"

Most sales people will get very excited when an owner or a manager shares his biggest challenges and how they are happening. Don't let that excitement ruin the situation. The key is not to push and shove your expertise or to be too quick to suggest that you have the best solution.

This is about listening. So stop talking now.

Follow the script by asking a time-and-temperature question. I say something like, "In that particular time you were talking about, on a scale of one to ten, how well did that work for you and your team in solving the issue?" Make sure you qualify the scale of one to ten. If they are a Steady personality, you may need to amend the scale by offering choices of one, five or ten.

Once you have a clear understanding of what is wrong and what they have tried, it's important to find out if they actually want to solve this challenge...if they think finding a solution is even worth the time and money.

I usually ask one or two questions. One goes like this, "What were you hoping someone like me could do to help?" Or, I might ask, "Have you given up trying to find a fix?"

Note to remember: Some prospects have decided not to pursue a solution or they have given up on trying to solve the problem. If that's the case, here's the key--bad news isn't like wine. It doesn't get better with time. If someone truly doesn't need your service, accept it. By asking the Agonizer Sequence questions, you will know because they will honestly tell you.

Believe them and stop the sales process here.

However, if they are still looking to fix the issue, keep moving forward.

Depending on the personality type of the prospect, I might ask, "What does your head tell you this issue is costing you or your company each month, or each week, or every year?" You may want to consider that the cost of this issue is not only figured in terms of money.

Money is only one way to measure things.

One prospect of mine said that money isn't the issue but the knot in her stomach was. When a prospect shares something like this on the phone, use a time and temperature question to delve deeper. You might say, "During those times when your stomach is in knots, on a scale of one to ten, where do you stand when you say it's a knot in your stomach?"

The cost could also be about time. We can make more money, but we cannot make more time. Make sure you understand how a prospect is measuring and quantifying the size and cost of this issue and if they are looking for your help.

What you need to succeed at this step in the process is to book an appointment. Don't try to sell or solve issues on the phone in this call. Your next step is to be invited in.

VOICE MAIL TIP

If body language makes up over two-thirds of communication, I want you to ask yourself this question:

How important is my tone and tempo on the phone when the person on the other end can't see me?

In a face-to-face meeting, tone and tempo is about 30 percent of communication. On the telephone, it's 90 percent. The spoken word is less than 10 percent. Please record your side of the conversation or voice mail. You must slow down, speak up, and follow a script.

Own the script. Practice your tone and tempo. It's not the same for each prospect. If they are speaking loudly or working as a Dominant personality, you have to speak up and match tone and tempo. Choose your words wisely. If you can master tone and tempo and follow our script, you'll have them at hello.

TAKE ACTION RIGHT NOW!

Agonizer Sequence. Powerful pain questions will have them dialing 911 for your help

- Let's pretend you have a Magic Marker. What would it take for you to be pleased with your progress?
- Use the zero technique of questioning. Repeat the last word the prospect says to you. If they end with "That seems like a lot", you ask, "A lot?"
- Ask for the client's time and temperature: on a scale of 1 to 10 how well is *that* working?
- Ask, "What were you thinking we could do?"
- Ask, "How much time, money, or energy is that costing you?"
- Say, "I get the feeling you are throwing in the towel. Is that the case?"

STEP 9

Invite Me In

APPOINTMENT-GETTER THAT STICKS LIKE GLUE

I recently consulted a group of nearly 50 cold calling agents in the Bay Area. As a team they made thousands of calls each week resulting in only a handful of actual appointments. To add insult to injury, those appointment were kept less than 6 percent of the time. That's a cancellation rate of nearly 94 percent! Their bosses had them playing a numbers game: make X number of calls, you'll get Y number of appointments. It was all about quantity and nothing about quality: getting a result—which in this case would have been an appointment not only booked, *but kept*.

You can understand why the motivation and general attitude of this team was at an all-time low They were aggravated with the training, frustrated with the demands of the sales manager, and in some cases ready to throw up their hands and start looking for a new career.

As you progress in my system, you discover that the real key is to make an appointment that sticks. You can use all the techniques in the world on the phone and during the call; however, if the prospect doesn't show for the scheduled appointment, the process is all for nothing.

Your goal needs to focus on making an appointment that sticks.

Think about the times when you have an appointment with your hair dresser, dentist, or some form of a medical specialist you have seen for many years. What is the likelihood of you canceling? It's between slim and none. You know that you'll have to wait another month to get in and, more importantly, you may even have to pay for the appointment even though you were a no-show. It will help you if your clients perceive that you have a fully booked appointment calendar. More to the point, start acting as if you are wanted in your industry. In other words, you want to appear to be booked solid until you truly are booked solid. When others perceive you this way, they will show more respect to you and for your time.

As sales people, we are eager to book any potential opening or fulfill any whim a prospect throws out at us. How about next week, how about now, how about next year, how about the end of the week? Your answer now is probably nearly always, "I can make that work!" The reason we say this is because we've worked so hard developing some sort of rapport and getting to the so-called next step of an appointment that we don't want to do anything to upset the proverbial apple cart. When you see my system and script to follow for the appointment-getter, my guess is, you'll be like most. Because you wouldn't like it used on yourself, or you just don't think it sounds right, you will not even try. I want you to ask this question out loud. How do you feel about your current system where nearly 90 percent of those who agree to an appointment never show up? And the worst part is you have no idea why. My system allows you to root out early why they might not show up, an early or pending objection to your potential deal, and more importantly, a way to show not only that you are booked solid, but that you are different from all the other so-called sales professionals who call.

My blueprint does two things that will set you apart from others in the field. First, it will demonstrate that you are not willing to eagerly slap an appointment together. It will also suggest that you are tuned in to what someone is really saying. Specifically, you recognize that a quick agreement to an appointment is likely code for, "I like you". Or, "I'm tired of you." Or, "If I act like I'm going to show up by saying yes to an appointment, I'll never have to deal with you again."

So, what's next after you have surmised it might seem like the right time to ask for the appointment? Here are the key steps:

1. Would it make sense to...

   "Would it make sense for you to invite me in and see if we can co-build a solution?"

   Remember the key here is we invite friends in and set appointments with sales people. That's why I specifically ask you if it would make sense to invite me in.

2. How would you like me to proceed? Pen or pencil?

   After you have determined a date and time to meet for the appointment, I ask the question, "Should I write that in pen or pencil?" It's a very simple question, but it is asking deeper down, "Are you going to keep this appointment with me or are you going to break it?" Note: This usually is the most difficult question sales people to ask. They are afraid that the answer might be pencil!

3. Do you see anything between ____ and ____...

   After I set a date that is in pen, I can now follow up with the next sequenced question that sounds like this: "Do you see anything between now and next Monday at 2 p.m. that will keep you from making our meeting?" This also allows you an opportunity to reschedule if there is some form of an illness or pending event that might make more sense to move the date.

4. My biggest fear ...

   If the date is set, I can now bring the future into the present by asking a very simple question. "My biggest fear is when we meet again, the problem might be solved, I might cost too much, or maybe you are just thinking I'm a good guy and will postpone the meeting. Is that just me, or is that the case?"

5. What did you like best about our call today?

   As I finish up, I want to make sure I don't sound like the typical sales person. I'll ask the next question along this line. "Oh by the way, before I go, what did you like best about our call today?" I'm looking for a buy sign or some form of coaching in terms of what worked and the prospect can also tell me what didn't work. As I'm completing the call, I also ask if they know anyone else who might need my service, and I repeat the date and time again. It's critical to not only follow up with an e-mail reminder or some version of a calendar accept-invite, but also a hand-written card.

TAKE ACTION RIGHT NOW!

Invite me in: The appointment-getter that sticks like glue!

- What's the next step after it appears they want to book an appointment?
- Would it make sense to ___________?
- Pen or ___________?
- Do you see anything between _____ and _____ that might change that?
- My biggest fear ___________.
- What did you like best about our call today?

WRAP UP

Putting It All Together

FEWER CALLS, MORE MONEY AND MORE TIME OFF

You've read this book. So what happens?

Typically, only about 3 to 9 percent of people who read and work on projects like this will ever take action. In other words, if they read the book, that's all that happens because they don't make any effort to apply what they learned. But you aren't like that. You have already beat the odds because most people who buy books like this one do not even finish reading the book. Surprisingly, 90 percent buy a book based on the cover and never go beyond chapter one. They'll just continue to do the same old behavior that keeps them stuck in the place where they are today. You aren't like that either.

I believe that since you've made it this far, you have the capacity to succeed in this difficult field because you care about improving and you know how to take action. The reason making cold calls works is because so few people do it. Most of the people who make an attempt at cold calls have no idea how to make the call correctly. You now have the tools, script ideas, and plan of attack. The rest is your behavior. By writing this book, I'm responsible to you, but, I'm not responsible for you.

Your first step is to take action. (Not tomorrow, not next week, but right now!)

How do you do that?

Go back to chapter one and follow the simple path that never leads to rejection. I don't want you to start by calling someone you don't know on a list. Start with a chance for success, by calling a current client and thanking them for their business and asking for help. If you're new to the job, call a former client, colleague or friend and follow the same way. Say, "Thanks for being a friend. Would you be willing to help me?"

Get yourself in the right frame of mind. Speaking of frame of mind, don't put all the pressure on yourself to make a sale. Think W.I.N. What I Need is a conversation or an appointment.

Make sure you focus on tone, tempo and personality type. I would encourage you to take some version of a DiSC personality assessment. Invest in yourself. You purchased this book, so go the extra mile and take an assessment. Create a chart with the DiSC profile and use the characters I describe to help you match the person on the other end of the line with tone, tempo, and personality style.

My success in both making cold calls and coaching cold calling techniques is based on voice quality, tone, tempo and understanding the personality of the prospects on the other end of the line. Remember, do not practice on prospects and clients. That's what I call sales malpractice. Practice on friends, family members and baristas at drive-throughs.

Get so good at what you do, people cannot ignore your skill.

Take time to work on the fun part: Expectations Interrupted. My clients have so much fun that they call me with good cold call news. They always say, "Hey, Dave, it's me. Did I catch you at a bad time?" Make that a part of your everyday vernacular every time you pick up the phone and call someone.

The Trojan Horse will help you to no longer be fearful of Gatekeepers. Remember, they really are nice people. They just have a job to do that we don't like. Their role's key description is to keep us out. So ask for them to help you in.

Oh, and by the way, what if they say no?

Well, practice. Say things like, "What could I have done better?" or my favorite "I don't suppose you know someone else who might need my service?"

From the movie "We Bought a Zoo" with Matt Damon, I have to tell you, "I promise you that with ten seconds of insane courage great things will happen to you." Ten seconds of insane courage will become a motto to live by in your cold call world. But also remember, some people you call may not be a fit for your business model. Decide what their real story is. Don't be afraid to ask who, what and where questions.

On days when your confidence wanes, use the following reminders to regroup:

- You don't have to like cold calls; you just need to schedule time to do it every day.
- Daily rhythm: how can I start out cold calls the right way? Call friends and family.

- Working through my biggest fears? All I need is an appointment or conversation to win.
- What is my personality type? What is my tone and tempo?
- Let's go to work and say something they are not expecting me to say (Expectation Interrupted).
- Someone answered. Now what do I do? Get the Gatekeeper to help you.
    - This sounds good, but what if they say no? (I needed practice so that call helped me work on my script).
    - This sounds great, but what if they say yes? (Here's the hard part--owning your Magic Script so it doesn't sound like a script. Its not the size of the part, but what you put into the part).
- How do I take them from "We're happy with what we have" to the point of "Please come and save me before our business dies?" The Agonizer Script is not only fun, it works to perfection.
    - 'Invite me in' is the secret to getting to first base. Don't get in a hurry and ask for a kiss goodnight just yet.

I wish I could tell you that once you master these techniques you'll never have another moment of concern. I can't tell you that. I can promise it gets easier. But your work is still difficult because sales is a difficult field. Here's the reason why I struggle with it. My parents, taught me things like don't talk to strangers and don't ask strangers for money. They also told me it wasn't nice to talk to people about how much money they made for a living. They said don't talk about dollars, period! As a kid, I used to get in a lot of trouble for answering the phone, especially after they said, "Don't answer it. We're not home. It's probably a sales person of some sort."

Now, my job is to pick up the phone, talk to strangers, ask them for money and talk about money. I suppose they think I'm a sales person of some sort. I can tell you, however, after I make the first call every day and use this system nonstop, I feel a lot better about myself, my business, and, more importantly, about the field of helping others. Now it's time for you to go out and control the call when "Dialing Strangers."

Oh, and by the way, I've mastered dialing strangers but I'd still never have the guts to talk to Shanell.

"This guy is a cold call rock star!"